I0419774

THE MYTHOLOGY OF NARCISSISM

SCHOLARLY ARTICLES BY PETER FRITZ WALTER

THE MYTHOLOGY
OF NARCISSISM

PATHOLOGY OF THE CONSUMER AGE

BY PETER FRITZ WALTER

Published by Sirius-C Media Galaxy LLC
Business Filings Incorporated
108 West 13th St., Wilmington, DE 19801

©2015 Peter Fritz Walter. Some rights reserved.

2020 Revised, Updated and Reformatted Edition.

Creative Commons Attribution 4.0 International License

The moral right of the author has been asserted

Set Trajan Pro and ITC Berkeley Oldstyle Std

Designed by Peter Fritz Walter

Publishing Categories
Psychology / Social Psychology

Publisher Contact Information
publisher@sirius-c-publishing.com
http://sirius-c-publishing.com

Author Contact Information
pfw@peterfritzwalter.com

About Dr. Peter Fritz Walter
http://peterfritzwalter.com

About the Author

Parallel to an international law career in Germany, Switzerland and the United States, Dr. Peter Fritz Walter (Pierre) focused upon fine art, cookery, astrology, musical performance, social sciences and humanities.

He started writing essays as an adolescent and received a high school award for creative writing and editorial work for the school magazine.

After finalizing his law diplomas, he graduated with an LL.M. in European Integration at Saarland University, Germany, and with a Doctor of Law title from University of Geneva, Switzerland, in 1987.

He then took courses in psychology at the University of Geneva and interviewed a number of psychotherapists in Lausanne and Geneva, Switzerland. His interest was intensified through a hypnotherapy with an Ericksonian American hypnotherapist in Lausanne. This led him to the recovery and healing of his inner child.

In 1986, he met the late French psychotherapist and child psychoanalyst Françoise Dolto (1908-1988) in Paris and interviewed her. A long correspondence followed up to their encounter which was considered by the curators of the Dolto Trust interesting enough to be published in a book alongside all of Dolto's other letter exchanges by Gallimard Publishers in Paris, in 2005.

After a second career as a corporate trainer and personal coach, Pierre retired as a full-time writer, philosopher and consultant.

His nonfiction books emphasize a systemic, holistic, cross-cultural and interdisciplinary perspective, while his fiction works and short stories focus upon education, philosophy, perennial wisdom, and the poetic formulation of an integrative worldview.

Pierre is a German-French bilingual native speaker and writes English as his 4th language after German, Latin and French. He also reads source literature for his research works in Spanish, Italian, Portuguese, and Dutch. In addition, Pierre has notions of Thai, Khmer, Chinese and Japanese.

All of Pierre's books are hand-crafted and self-published, designed by the author. Pierre publishes via his Delaware company, Sirius-C Media Galaxy LLC, and under the imprints of IPUBLICA and SCM (Sirius-C Media).

CONTENTS

The secret of healing narcissism is not to heal it at all, but to listen to it. (...) I am stuff. I am made up of things and qualities, and in loving these things I love myself.

—THOMAS MOORE, CARE OF THE SOUL (1994)

INTRODUCTION

Why Studying Narcissism?

I have learnt about narcissism early in life, in my twenties, at first in the 1970s through some of the books by Sigmund Freund and Wilhelm Reich and later, more thoroughly, through the books of Alice Miller and Alexander Lowen, back in the 1980s.

> —See, for example, Alexander Lowen, Narcissism: Denial of the True Self (1983) and Alice Miller, The Drama of the Gifted Child: In Search for the True Self (1996) as well as Thou Shalt Not Be Aware: Society's Betrayal of the Child (1998).

Both psychiatrists are since long years specialized on narcissism and it was through their unique input and unwavering efforts that today the seriousness of the narcissistic affliction has been recognized in mainstream psychiatry.

This was namely not the case when they started out to publish on this matter, back in the 1970s. To be true, at that time, narcissism was as good as overlooked in psychiatry, and was not held to be a serious affliction.

Today, while health care professionals recognize the seriousness of narcissism as a psychiatric disorder, the general public maintains a state of confusion and misinformation about the very term and the nature of the narcissistic affliction that I have hardly seen for any other psychiatric problem.

It is often wrongly assumed that narcissism means to overly love oneself! If that was so, there would not be a problem at all with narcissism. But narcissism is the very contrary of love of oneself, it is the very denial of love of oneself—and that makes that it's a problem.

CHAPTER ONE

What is Narcissism?

THE OVERALL BEHAVIOR PATTERN

Perhaps it was a chance that I never bothered too much about the term itself, as it is confusing and misleads many people. There is about no other subject where the clash between professional knowledge and the half-knowledge of lay persons is so large as with narcissism. Everybody seems to know what narcissism means, but when you inquire further, you see that people maintain the strangest misconceptions about it.

Most people have heard about the ancient myth of Narcissus that is at the origin of the term narcissism. But what does this myth tell us? Here is where the misconceptions start. Most people somehow got a scarce idea and extrapolate from the little knowledge they got, and the result is a standard answer like:

—Oh yes, this strange guy who looked in the water and saw his mirror! That guy loved himself too much, he was fallen in love with himself …

And then they go concluding narcissism was a hang-up of people who 'love themselves too much,' who are fixated upon their own self-image, who are fallen in love with themselves.

—These people just love only themselves, they have no reception antennas for other people, they are selfish and even their erotic love is turned toward their own person, instead of being turned toward others.

Needless to say that all of this is sheer nonsense. The very contrary is true.

Narcissism is a pathology where the person, through deep hurt suffered early in life, is unable to love himself or herself, and thus lacks even a basic level of self-love. And what is worse with this affliction is that the true self of the person, their self identity, their feeling self, their I-AM, and also their body image, have been buried deep down in the unconscious. The result is that narcissistic people do not know who they are or, as it is expressed in psychiatry, they deny their true self.

This denial of their own intrinsic being, their character, their values and oddities, their depth and dignity is what lets them appear like shadow dancers.

They are generally fluent talkers and take up new ideas quickly, but they do not integrate novelty, because there is nothing they could integrate it into, as they are out of touch with their true identity, the fertile soil of their human nature, their grounding.

I use to call them for this reason 'narcissistic comedians,' as they actually behave as if being on stage, as if life was a huge stage where everybody performs a role—but where nobody plays the role of himself or herself, but always another. A plays B, B plays C, C plays A. But life normally is that A plays A, B plays B and C plays C.

People who suffer from narcissism tend to appear aloof, they appear to float, as if their feet never touched the ground beneath. There is often also something Peter-Pan like about them, something fragile and strangely youthful, often accompanied by a sunshine smile that seems to suggest that they know no sadness; while in truth, they are the saddest people on earth, only that they can't even feel their sadness, alienated as they are from their feelings, because they have repressed their deepest emotions.

In exchanges with narcissists I also found that they often deny the reality of emotions, trying to grasp all of reality with their pure intellect—that usually works brilliantly well. But that makes that they are truly alienated from humanity because they more or less consciously discard the irrational out of the world. For them, all must be rational, clear and straight, and they tend to condemn irrationality in people, out of touch as they are with their own irrationality.

We humans are at times rational and at times irrational. We are as good as never only rational or only irrational; we are a mix of many qualities and oddities, and it's our vivid emotions that bring the necessary kaleidoscopic change in our lives so that we are not for too long rational and not for too long irrational. But for the narcissist there has to be only rationality, and all the rest is as it were human weakness …

And as they judge what is most extraordinary in the human to be weakness, they fatally remain with that weakness and cannot realize their divine potential. The natives would say that these people have lost their soul.

HOW TO IDENTIFY NARCISSISM?

You can identify rather quickly if you suffer from a narcissistic fixation or not. Simply check if you *play yourself* in your life, or if you are yourself. Check if you play a role that fakes it is you. Then, when you ask this question and it rings like 'But who am I?,' you are getting on the right track. When that question feels odd and strange because somehow you have never asked who you are, and if in the game of life you as good as never play the Me-card, then you know you have a problem with narcissism.

Another reality check would be the obsessional idea to be altruistic and 'always good' to others, to a point of self-forgetfulness. Rings true? Why should you forget about yourself? You feel it's a 'moral duty' to be always concerned about others, while putting yourself behind? No, it's not. But you probably have a hangup with narcissism, as you are constantly denying your own self, replacing the vacuum at need with person A, friend B or relative C that you have to help out, to save from bad luck, rape or incest, to heal, to comfort, to look after, to console, to protect, and so on.

Narcissism is really not a complicated thing and it's not difficult to grasp. It has been made difficult to understand through popular psychology that loves to use strange terms and indulges in express-ing simple facts in a simple way. For example, it's much more difficult to explain what neurosis is or psychosis than to say what narcissism means and what makes persons afflicted with narcissism suffer so much in life. They really suffer!

Narcissism is not a party affliction, not a gentleman disease, and not an outflow of vanity, while it is often belittled as such. Narcissism is an affliction serious enough to be put on priority by most of today's psychiatric services.

For when you're out of touch with yourself and your deepest emotions, you live a life that is not yours, you live an 'empty life.' This inner vacuum, this emptiness when it's constant, is something that can trigger other serious afflictions such as substance abuse, chain smoking, depression, chronic fatigue, alcoholism, anxiety, phobias, and sexual obsessions, aggression and perversion.

It also can trigger somatizations, which means that the body gets ill for reasons that are not physiological, but psychological.

CHAPTER TWO

Narcissism and Soul

A nother corner of the literature on narcissism is what spiritual-minded people say about it. Their terminology is different, and that unfortunately also contributes to the general confusion about narcissism.

I have in mind a particularly successful and brilliant author, Thomas Moore, whose most famous bestselling book, *Care of the Soul (1994)*, is not a psychiatric manual for healing narcissism. It is a philosophical study for understanding the roots of narcissism both in our culture and individually, in our lives.

But the problem is one of terminology. Moore speaks of soul and of lacking soul when he describes narcissism. His ideas are brilliant, and he points the finger on the wound when he says that narcissism cannot be healed through pushing the person into a growth cycle or by otherwise suggesting the person 'to grow up.' Thomas more writes:

> Narcissism has no soul. In narcissism we take away the soul's substance, its weight and importance, and reduce it to an echo of our own thoughts. There is no such thing as the soul. We say. It is only the brain going through its electrical and chemical changes. Or it is only behavior. Or it is only memory and conditioning. In our social narcissism, we also dismiss the soul as irrelevant. We can prepare a city or national budget, but leave the needs of the soul untended. Narcissism will not give its power to anything as nymphlike as the soul. (Id., 58-59)

I have coached narcissistic and highly problematic individuals over the Internet, free of charge, for a period of almost ten years, considering this as the 'social' part of my mission as a coach, and I found invariably that they wait for society to accept them, instead of doing the first step and accept themselves! Moore explains:

> What the narcissist does not understand is that the self-acceptance he craves can't be forced or manufactured. It has to be discovered, in a place more introverted than the usual haunts of the

narcissist. There has to be some inner questioning, and maybe even confusion. (Id., 60-61)

And I made an astonishing discovery. I had myself a narcissism problem over many years, starting
in my childhood, and it was not cured with a hypnotherapy, but I could cure it subsequently, virtual-
ly by 'talking to the trees.' It was almost fifteen
years ago when, living in the Provence, I took the
habit to go for night walks, when I would address
speech to some of the trees in a huge alley with sycamores.

There were three huge sycamores I felt sponta-
neously attracted to, and what I would do, late
enough so that no cars would pass by, was to put
my right hand firmly against the trunk of the tree,
and talk to the tree, either by thinking or by whis-
pering my ideas.

Now, what happened to my surprise was that
not only was I greatly energized through this
unique kind of conversation, to a point to not being tired when coming home, but also to have
dreams where the tree was talking back to me. And

I learnt amazing depths of wisdom from these dreams!

Now, I was of course very surprised when I found the following passage in *Care of the Soul* (1994):

> I suspect that this is a very concrete part of curing narcissism—talking to the trees. By engaging the so-called 'inanimate' world in dialogue, we are acknowledging its soul. Not all consciousness is human. That in itself is a narcissistic belief. (Id., 61)

And indeed, through my talking to the trees, I felt a sudden interest in shamanism and went on a spiritual quest that took me several years. I engaged in a tedious research about shamanism and went to Ecuador, in 2004, to drink the traditional sacred Ayahuasca brew.

I left this initiation completely transformed, for I regained the whole range of magical beliefs I fostered as a child, and this really has completely healed the narcissistic condition.

Now, Thomas Moore has put a particular stress in this book on the danger of collective narcissism and he investigates deeply in the culture of the United States of America, to identify it as a narcissistic culture par excellence. Moore writes:

> Nations, as well as individuals, can go through this initiation. America has a great longing to be the New World of opportunity and a moral beacon for the world. It longs to fulfill these narcissistic images of itself. At the same time it is painful to realize the distance between the reality and that image. America's narcissism is strong. It is paraded before the world. If we were to put the nation on the couch, we might discover that narcissism is its most obvious symptom. And yet that narcissism holds the promise that this all-important myth can find its way into life. In other words, America's narcissism is its refined puer spirit of genuine new vision. The trick is to find a way to that water of transformation where hard self-absorption turns into loving dialogue with the world. (Id., 62)

When we look at how present-day America, with its strongly narcissistic government, faces this 'loving dialogue,' we see that the puer spirit is indeed very strong. Not only is it strong but Americans somehow like to choose their presidents among puer personalities, and that may one day result in a fatal outcome!

Mature cultures choose mature leaders, senior personalities, people who have grown out from the cradle or from an adolescence where Peter Pan is the dominating archetype.

And it is very interesting that Moore also notes that curing narcissism involves an expansion of boundaries:

> Narcissus becomes able to love himself only when he learns to love that self as an object. He now has a view of himself as someone else. This is not ego loving ego; this is ego loving the soul, loving a face the soul presents. We might say that the cure for narcissism is to move from love of self, which always has a hint of narcissism in it, to love of one's deep soul. Or, to put it another way, narcissism breaking up invites us to expand the boundaries of who we think we are. (Id., 63)

And here again, when we look at present-day reality in the United States, boundary-dissolving substances, from DMT, over LSD to Marijuana have all been declared illegal, which shows the degree of narcissism at the top government level in the enlightened nation. Only that the light seems to come from the wrong source.

And the enlightened nation is an action nation. All is action. The major coach-actor of the nation, Anthony Robbins, performs in shorts, jumping around like a school boy. When all is action, everybody is an actor. Not himself. And everybody acts out his or her life, instead of living it.

This timelessness of the nation, in the sense of 'never having time,' which is embodied in its business values, business standing for busyness, is one of the symptoms of its cultural narcissism that is not a present-day phenomenon. The action-nation was born in New England, in the 18th century. When there is no more time, there is no more soul. Moore explains:

> A neurotic narcissism won't allow the time needed to stop, reflect, and see the many emotions, memories, wishes, fantasies, desires, and fears that make up the materials of the soul. As a result, the narcissistic person becomes fixed on a single idea of who he is, and other possibilities are automatically rejected. (Id., 67)

Peter Pan resisted to grow up. And astonishingly enough, Thomas Moore writes that growing-up is not a cure for narcissism, in the contrary:

But the solution of narcissism is not growing up. On the contrary, the solution to narcissism is to give the myth as much realization as possible, to the point where a tiny bud appears indicating the flowering of personality through its narcissism. (...) Narcissism is a condition in which a person does not love himself. This failure in love comes through as its opposite because the person tries so hard to find self-acceptance. The complex reveals itself in the all-too-obvious effort and exaggeration. It's clear to all around that narcissism's love is shallow. We know instinctively that someone who talks about himself all the time must not have a very strong sense of self. To the individual caught up in this myth, the failure to find self-love is felt as a kind of masochism, and, whenever masochism comes into play, a sadistic element is not far behind. The two attitudes are polar elements in a split power archetype. (Id., 71)

When we apply this truth to the Peter Pan nation, we learn that we have to let them run where they run and let them break even more glass everywhere in the world, right? I am not sure if Thomas Moore wanted to say that because once of a sudden, after having expanded into collective narcissism, he again speaks of the individual.

But our daily news about the hero culture really seem to suggest that Moore's analysis of collective narcissism, that is shared by number of depth psy-chologists, would lead to an abysmal accumulation of Peter-Pan like acts, performed as a nation-nar-cissist on the world at large, in order to gain depth. I am not so sure if this psychological solution will work out politically, because even the most opti-mistic of Peter Pans around in the great nation may get a hint of stretching the bow too much … and the international repercussions may not permit Pe-ter Pan to continue his puer game infinitely …

Anyway, from the soul perspective, and leaving political realities untouched, Thomas Moore writes:

> The secret of healing narcissism is not to heal it at all, but to listen to it. (…) I am stuff. I am made up of things and qualities, and in loving these things I love myself. (Id., 73)

This is in accordance with a general soul-based healing approach that was the prevalent approach to healing during the Middle-Ages and the Renais-sance. Moore writes:

> Robert Burton in his massive self-help book of the seventeenth century The Anatomy of Melan-choly, says there is only one cure for the melan-

cholic sickness of love: enter into it with aban-
don. Some authors today argue that romantic
love is such an illusion that we need to distrust
it and keep our wits about us so that we are not
led astray. But warnings like this betray a distrust of the soul. (Id., 81)

CHAPTER THREE

The Origin of Narcissism

In order to realize our personal identity and become whole human beings, we have to be able, still in childhood, to form an original personal identity. This is however impossible if we are reared by narcissistic parents, those namely that are indifferent to the unique person of the child they have brought to life.

Narcissistic education is one of indoctrination going together with gradually alienating children from their bodies. The most effective way to indoctrinate children with a certain culture is to implant in their mind a deeply rooted doubt about who they are. This doubt which creates a vacuum will then be filled with magic formulas such as 'Be not what you are!'

The next step is to force the child to play roles in order to please their parents. The main role in this drama which is the *Drama of the Gifted Child*, as Alice Miller called it, is the role of the child as father or mother of their own parents.

This education that I use to call 'rearing narcissistic comedians,' is very common in what I came to call, for this very reason, *Oedipal Culture*.

—My critique of Oedipal Culture is inextricably woven with my critique of Sigmund Freud's cultural concept of the Oedipus Complex. See Peter Fritz Walter, Normative Psychoanalysis: How the Oedipal Dogma Shapes Consumer Culture (Scholarly Articles Vol. 14), 2015/2017.

This is why narcissism is rampant in Western nations, especially in the United States.

However, there are few researchers who see that the main etiology for narcissism is to be found in our child-rearing paradigm. Those who do, such as Alice Miller or Alexander Lowen, are not representing mainstream psychology, despite the brilliance of their work. They have, inter alia, found that education that typically leads to narcissism is rich in inventing and executing magic formulas that are given to the child for so-called 'good education' but that are in reality perverting hypnotic injunctions. Some of these are 'Hypnotic Injunctions Recognized by TA (Transactional Analysis).'

These injunctions have been found by TA as highly destructive for the child's emotional, cognitive, motor, skill and sexual development. They are voiced often nonverbally, through implication, through examples given, through confused and imprecise language, through reproaches and through comparisons that may or not be true.

- Be adaptable and flexible until self-alienation;

- Never be yourself in front of your parents;

- Be not child-like, but adult-like;

- Be mature in immaturity;

- Understand what your parents don't understand;

- Be logical and uncomplicated;

- Respect your parents while disrespecting yourself;

- Mistrust your intuition;

▶   Follow authority without questioning.

I see another etiology of narcissism in lacking primary symbiosis between mother and infant during the first eighteen months after birth. Regularly, with mothers who themselves suffer from narcissism, clinical research found a reduction or total absence of eye contact between mother and child, absence of breast-feeding or when the breast is given, the mother feels revulsion, disgust or aggression toward the child; in addition, such mothers tend to be hostile to the child's first steps into autonomy, thereby creating in the child a pathological clinging-behavior that has very nasty consequences later on in the development of the child and young adult.

Often what happens in such relationships is that the mother manipulates the child into a real codependence where she projects her longings for love, that remain unfulfilled in the partner relation, upon the child. This then in many cases leads to emotional abuse, and on the level of the child, a perversion of their psychosexual orientation into gerontophilia.

Narcissism thus is often the inevitable result of emotional abuse suffered in early childhood, and that fact may help to understand the gravity of the affliction of narcissism.

What this results in is that the person later unconsciously tries to heal the lacking primary fusion by repeated pseudo-symbiotic relationships, which are relationships where love is replaced by dependency or confused with dependency. However, since those persons that are invested with that role of ersatz mothers and fathers can never give the lacking primary fusion, disappointment and depression will invariably ensue in those relations.

Narcissism is an inevitable by-product of patriarchy, and its etiology is wrong relating: wrong relating to self, wrong relating to others. It is built on what Joseph Campbell called the 'solar worldview' and ignores the many shadows of the soul—and thereby ignores its own shadow.

Narcissists, therefore, are tragic figures. They are tragic in the sense that they run into the abyss without the slightest idea of what they are doing because they are not grounded and have their feet in the air, like the *Fool* of the Tarot. They are lunatics, because they have not integrated their own Luna, their Moon energy.

They are the eternal Peter Pan's of sunshine movies, and present themselves to the public smiling, broadly smiling, most of the time, but in haphazard moments you see their true face—while they themselves ignore it.

CHAPTER FOUR

The Performance Paradigm

We have seen that narcissism can be both an individual affliction and a cultural phenomenon, and has become increasingly 'cultural' or 'collective' with the birth of the consumer paradigm and mass production, automated fabrication and streamlined standard education that stresses the need for un-privileged access to consumption.

In the last chapter of this article, I would like to discuss an area of cultural narcissism that is not yet discovered by the psychiatric, nor even the popular psychology literature, perhaps because it is more subtle and less obvious a fact of life in post-modern consumer society.

I am talking about the bias between creating and performing. To anticipate the outcome of my analysis, I am saying that creating is not what our society rewards and encourages, but performing. Not the creator is anymore the hero, but the performer, not the originator but the imitator, not the creative artist but the recreative artist. Why? Because what is the order of the day is not assimilation of culture, nor cultural advancement, but mere recreation, which is more properly called entertainment.

What is entertainment? A form of distraction, not contemplation, and thereby a way of of dissipating energy instead of accumulating energy.

I will try in this last part of my article to give some flesh to this idea, and also, to illustrate it with some real-life examples. Let me first try to explain the perhaps historical roots of what in classical music is called the 'performance paradigm.'

It all started at the times of Mozart and Beethoven, and especially Chopin and Liszt, when not, as before, the pianists played their own works, but became mere virtuosos who played, as it is today, compositions they would not be able to compose in the first place. The change came slowly and gradually, perhaps at around the time of Josef Hofmann (1876-1957), who set in motion a totally new paradigm. It was from that time no more the composer who plays his works, and a few others in between, but the pianist virtuoso, who played 'a repertoire,' a choice of music, and where he or she rather often used to 'adapt' the piece to their own stretch of hands, or would bluntly rewrite a part of the score for 'better pleasing the public.'

It was common from about that time that pianists wore special clothes and displayed distinct mannerisms to attract the attention of the public, if they were not outright piano acrobats.

With the performer paradigm replacing the creator paradigm, the whole musical world changed, and the ultimate results we see today must sadden the true music lover.

At the same time, the tendency set in that the performance aspects of a composition were validated higher than the composition itself. For example, it was very common at that time to play a non-legato ostinato passage in a sonata or fantasy in octaves, thereby duplicating the notes to play, but at the same time, reinforcing the sound. It was rather seldom questioned if so doing was actually justified by the composer's intention.

Here is a good example of this vision of musical performance of that time, by an eminent virtuoso of that time, Ignaz Moscheles (1794-1880), himself a contemporary of Meyerbeer, Hummel, Kalkbrenner, Cramer, Herz and Weber, who all inscribed into that early virtuoso tradition.

Harold C. Schonberg reports in his book *The Great Pianists (1963/1987)* that Moscheles once wrote in 1838, when pondering the new music:

> I play the new music of the four modern heroes, Thalberg, Chopin, Henselt and Liszt, and find their chief effects lie in passages requiring a large grasp and stretch of finger, such as the peculiar build of their hands enables them to execute. I grasp less, but then I am not of a grasping school. With all my admiration for Beethoven, I cannot forget Mozart, Cramer and Hummel. Have they not written much that is noble, with which I have been familiar from early years? Just now the new manner finds more favor, and I endeavor to pursue the middle

course between the two schools, by never
shrinking from any difficulty, never despising
the new effects, and withal retaining the best
elements of the old traditions.

Moscheles believed that music had reached its Golden Age during the period Bach to Beethoven, and was suspicious of the virtuoso performance paradigm as it was shown exemplarily by Chopin, Wagner, Liszt, Busoni, Godowsky and Berlioz.

Interestingly enough, one of the greatest exponents of the virtuoso paradigm, Franz Liszt (1811-1886), whose real Hungarian name was *Franz Ritter von Liszt-Ferenc*, was himself not a virtuoso in the sense that he was tastelessly modifying compositions not his own, to fit them to his own gusto. It was long unknown to what point Liszt was actually in this respect a man of the 20th century, who deeply respected the original score and intention of the composer, a fact that was mainly brought to our knowledge by one of the greatest Liszt interprets ever on this globe, the late Chilean pianist and nobleman Claudio Arrau (1903-1991).

Arrau said in several interviews with Chilean television that Liszt was a person very much ahead of his time and that his musical understanding was flawless; and against the myth of Liszt as a ruthless acrobatic piano executioner, who pays little attention to the score, Arrau forwarded the subtle image of Liszt as a person who was meticulous in his intention to reproduce the original vision of the composer in its finest details.

While Liszt, in accordance with the romantic tradition, was often transcribing music not originally composed for the piano, he even then tried to follow the composer's intention up into the finest details.

Now, the performance paradigm is what came upon us through this 18th and 19th century musical tradition, and we see its effects today aggrandized in many ways. For example, the flow of information to handle gets larger with every day, just for actually using all the wonderful features technology offers us in this modern culture. What strikes our consciousness these days is the question how people are going to handle this immense, undaunted information flow without actually turning mad, by a total breakdown of the nervous system?

The results are that the culture is going to change at a level even more drastic than we can imagine these days. Children grow up with computers they can touch while they have lost touch with their peers and parents; touch becomes widely part of the tech culture, and is unrooted from nature where it was primal first, and for very precise reasons.

The 'lack of time' phenomenon as a cultural obsession takes hold of people's intimate lives where with men, it turns the spiral toward large-scale impotence, as shown by newest sex research in Germany, because of the conception of sex as performance, to fit it in the performance culture—while sex originally had nothing to do with performing something. But that is how all our basic life functions get molded into the corporate culture for being validated under the consumer paradigm.

What can possibly be the future of the classical music, or acoustic music performance paradigm?

I see a dim picture here as young people excel on their synthesizers and keyboards they can use even in the night, with headphones, and can plug into their laptops and iPhones, transmitting their creations directly over the Web. Pianos are especially bulky and the pianist needs a heavy investment for a piano and the money to pay for a high-class apartment or single house, because the 'noise' disturbs others. (I was thrown out of the apartment of my mother, had to do a court action and lost it, when I was 22 years old, which added on to my brilliantly eloquent 'classical music trauma').

Prices for music constantly drop for classical, and rise for rock and pop, and some popular jazz, and even for new age when the artist is popular. So what is the future of the classical arts?

As the music management has largely assigned the classical scene to the bourgeoisie of old style, as this bourgeoisie is currently going to be replaced by a high-tech, and efficiency-prone new elite composed of very IT-literate men and women, I see black for the classical scene of old style, with its expensive operas and concert halls.

The international handphone technology demonstrates that modern strategies of business deployment may simply bypass any of the older systems, invalidating the former ways of doing in a matter of years. While still about a decade and a half ago the German government invested millions of euro to put all the phone line system to copper lining, which is very expensive, in Asia or Africa, such expenses have never been made. All there is simply wireless, while the quality is of course lousy but nobody complains about it, because they don't know any better. So, that means, when you apply that to our culture, that the development of all of it will be nonlinear, not following the traditional ways of doing things.

I see a dim future for the soul values of classical music because all will be transited toward 'narcissistic' performance with the virtuoso as the prime laureate, leaving the composer in the shadow. Young pianists today may do all of their promotion, using Youtube, their own web sites, iTunes and whatever and yet the audience is constantly shrinking.

Still in the times of my own youth, some forty years ago, it was the older generation who was interested in classical. I was among my peers the only one who liked classical music of any kind. Today, this old generation is basically all dead, and that means the audience is shifting greatly. The young people also if ever they want to hear a classical will not pay for it but watch it on free video channels such as Youtube, which means they are using second hand resources because they ignore the power of a first-hand life, as I call it. The whole culture will shift toward second-hand productions where the originality of an artist is lesser and lesser a factor that people want to consider. All this means that pianists today tend to diversify their repertoire in order to be prepared and ready to strike, the day when they see a certain type of music getting popular, and then specialize in it.

But, of course, the narcissism paradigm is not exclusive to classical music, but also an intrinsic part of the jazz culture, where it's stringently more the performer who is validated, applauded and lauded, than the composition itself. Actually the composition has hardly any value by itself which is metaphorically very well demonstrated by the fact that jazz compositions habitually figure in so-called 'fake books' as simple musical lines that are annotated with a code language, similar to the 'basso continuo' known in Baroque music, which marks and underlines the harmonization of the piece. It is then up to the skill of the jazz musician to 'write out' this code according to valid principles of musical composition.

I find the wordplay immensely suggestive, for what is content of a 'fake book' is after all fake, when considered in plain English.

So that would mean that the composition, in total alignment with the narcissistic consumer culture, has no more value, and hence, the composer has no more value, but solely the performer, because it's the latter that was declared as the cultural hero, because 'performance is better than composition,' exactly as in our culture 'violence is better than sex.'

BIBLIOGRAPHY

Contextual Bibliography

ARIÈS, PHILIPPE

Centuries of Childhood
NEW YORK: VINTAGE BOOKS, 1962

ARNTZ, WILLIAM & CHASSE, BETSY

What the Bleep Do We Know
20TH CENTURY FOX, 2005 (DVD)

Down The Rabbit Hole Quantum Edition
20TH CENTURY FOX, 2006 (3 DVD SET)

COVITZ, JOEL

Emotional Child Abuse
THE FAMILY CURSE
BOSTON: SIGO PRESS, 1986

DeMause, Lloyd

The History of Childhood
New York, 1974

Foundations of Psychohistory
New York: Creative Roots, 1982

Diamond, Stephen A., May, Rollo

Anger, Madness, and the Daimonic
The Psychological Genesis of Violence, Evil and Creativity
New York: State University of New York Press, 1999

DiCarlo, Russell E. (Ed.)

Towards A New World View
Conversations at the Leading Edge
Erie, PA: Epic Publishing, 1996

Dolto, Françoise

La Cause des Enfants
Paris: Laffont, 1985

Psychanalyse et Pédiatrie
Paris: Seuil, 1971

Séminaire de Psychanalyse d'Enfants, 1
Paris: Seuil, 1982

Séminaire de Psychanalyse d'Enfants, 2
PARIS: SEUIL, 1985

Séminaire de Psychanalyse d'Enfants, 3
PARIS: SEUIL, 1988

L'évangile au risque de la psychanalyse
PARIS: SEUIL, 1980

EISLER, RIANE

The Chalice and the Blade
OUR HISTORY, OUR FUTURE
SAN FRANCISCO: HARPER & ROW, 1995

Sacred Pleasure: Sex, Myth and the Politics of the Body
NEW PATHS TO POWER AND LOVE
SAN FRANCISCO: HARPER & ROW, 1996

The Partnership Way
NEW TOOLS FOR LIVING AND LEARNING
WITH DAVID LOYE
BRANDON, VT: HOLISTIC EDUCATION PRESS, 1998

The Real Wealth of Nations
CREATING A CARING ECONOMICS
SAN FRANCISCO: BERRETT-KOEHLER PUBLISHERS, 2008

ELLIS, HAVELOCK

Sexual Inversion
REPUBLISHED
NEW YORK: UNIVERSITY PRESS OF THE PACIFIC, 2001
ORIGINALLY PUBLISHED IN 1897

The Sexual Impulse in Women
REPUBLISHED
NEW YORK: UNIVERSITY PRESS OF THE PACIFIC, 2001
ORIGINALLY PUBLISHED IN 1903

The Dance of Life
NEW YORK: GREENWOOD PRESS REPRINT EDITION, 1973
ORIGINALLY PUBLISHED IN 1923

ELWIN, V.

The Muria and their Ghotul
BOMBAY: OXFORD UNIVERSITY PRESS, 1947

ERICKSON, MILTON H.

My Voice Will Go With You
THE TEACHING TALES OF MILTON H. ERICKSON
BY SIDNEY ROSEN (ED.)
NEW YORK: NORTON & CO., 1991

Complete Works 1.0, CD-ROM
NEW YORK: MILTON H. ERICKSON FOUNDATION, 2001

FREUD, SIGMUND

The Interpretation of Dreams
NEW YORK: AVON, REISSUE EDITION, 1980
AND IN: THE STANDARD EDITION OF THE COMPLETE PSYCHOLOGICAL
WORKS OF SIGMUND FREUD , (24 VOLUMES) ED. BY JAMES STRACHEY
NEW YORK: W. W. NORTON & COMPANY, 1976

Totem and Taboo
NEW YORK: ROUTLEDGE, 1999
ORIGINALLY PUBLISHED IN 1913

FROMM, ERICH

The Anatomy of Human Destructiveness
NEW YORK: OWL BOOK, 1992
ORIGINALLY PUBLISHED IN 1973

Escape from Freedom
NEW YORK: OWL BOOKS, 1994
ORIGINALLY PUBLISHED IN 1941
TO HAVE OR TO BE
NEW YORK: CONTINUUM INTERNATIONAL PUBLISHING, 1996
ORIGINALLY PUBLISHED IN 1976

The Art of Loving
NEW YORK: HARPERPERENNIAL, 2000
ORIGINALLY PUBLISHED IN 1956

GOLEMAN, DANIEL

Emotional Intelligence
NEW YORK, BANTAM BOOKS, 1995

GORDON, ROSEMARY

Pedophilia: Normal and Abnormal
IN: KRAEMER, THE FORBIDDEN LOVE
LONDON, 1976

GOSWAMI, AMIT

The Self-Aware Universe
HOW CONSCIOUSNESS CREATES THE MATERIAL WORLD
NEW YORK: TARCHER/PUTNAM, 1995

GROTH, A. NICHOLAS

Men Who Rape
THE PSYCHOLOGY OF THE OFFENDER
NEW YORK: PERSEUS PUBLISHING, 1980

HAMEROFF, NEWBERG, WOOLF, BIERMAN

Consciousness
20 SCIENTISTS INTERVIEWED
DIRECTOR: GREGORY ALSBURY
5 DVD BOX SET, 540 MIN.
NEW YORK: ALSBURY FILMS, 2003

JAMES, WILLIAM

Writings 1902-1910
THE VARIETIES OF RELIGIOUS EXPERIENCE / PRAGMATISM / A PLURALISTIC UNI-
VERSE / THE MEANING OF TRUTH / SOME PROBLEMS OF PHILOSOPHY / ESSAYS
NEW YORK: LIBRARY OF AMERICA, 1988

JUNG, CARL GUSTAV

Archetypes of the Collective Unconscious
IN: THE BASIC WRITINGS OF C.G. JUNG
NEW YORK: THE MODERN LIBRARY, 1959, 358-407

Collected Works
NEW YORK, 1959

On the Nature of the Psyche
IN: THE BASIC WRITINGS OF C.G. JUNG
NEW YORK: THE MODERN LIBRARY, 1959, 47-133

Psychological Types
COLLECTED WRITINGS, VOL. 6
PRINCETON: PRINCETON UNIVERSITY PRESS, 1971

Psychology and Religion
IN: THE BASIC WRITINGS OF C.G. JUNG
NEW YORK: THE MODERN LIBRARY, 1959, 582-655

Religious and Psychological Problems of Alchemy
IN: THE BASIC WRITINGS OF C.G. JUNG
NEW YORK: THE MODERN LIBRARY, 1959, 537-581

The Basic Writings of C.G. Jung
NEW YORK: THE MODERN LIBRARY, 1959

The Development of Personality
COLLECTED WRITINGS, VOL. 17
PRINCETON: PRINCETON UNIVERSITY PRESS, 1954

The Meaning and Significance of Dreams
BOSTON: SIGO PRESS, 1991

The Myth of the Divine Child
IN: ESSAYS ON A SCIENCE OF MYTHOLOGY
PRINCETON, N.J.: PRINCETON UNIVERSITY PRESS BOLLINGEN
SERIES XXII, 1969. (WITH KARL KERENYI)

Two Essays on Analytical Psychology
COLLECTED WRITINGS, VOL. 7
PRINCETON: PRINCETON UNIVERSITY PRESS, 1972
FIRST PUBLISHED BY ROUTLEDGE & KEGAN PAUL, LTD., 1953

KLEIN, MELANIE

Love, Guilt and Reparation, and Other Works 1921-1945
NEW YORK: FREE PRESS, 1984
(REISSUE EDITION)

Envy and Gratitude and Other Works 1946-1963
NEW YORK: FREE PRESS, 2002
(REISSUE EDITION)

KOESTLER, ARTHUR

The Act of Creation
NEW YORK: PENGUIN ARKANA, 1989.
ORIGINALLY PUBLISHED IN 1964

KRISHNAMURTI, J.

Freedom From The Known
SAN FRANCISCO: HARPER & ROW, 1969

The First and Last Freedom
SAN FRANCISCO: HARPER & ROW, 1975

Education and the Significance of Life
LONDON: VICTOR GOLLANCZ, 1978

CONTEXTUAL BIBLIOGRAPHY

Commentaries on Living
FIRST SERIES
LONDON: VICTOR GOLLANCZ, 1985

Commentaries on Living
SECOND SERIES
LONDON: VICTOR GOLLANCZ, 1986

Krishnamurti's Journal
LONDON: VICTOR GOLLANCZ, 1987

Krishnamurti's Notebook
LONDON: VICTOR GOLLANCZ, 1986

Beyond Violence
LONDON: VICTOR GOLLANCZ, 1985

Beginnings of Learning
NEW YORK: PENGUIN, 1986

The Penguin Krishnamurti Reader
NEW YORK: PENGUIN, 1987

On God
SAN FRANCISCO: HARPER & ROW, 1992

On Fear
SAN FRANCISCO: HARPER & ROW, 1995

The Essential Krishnamurti
SAN FRANCISCO: HARPER & ROW, 1996

The Ending of Time
WITH DR. DAVID BOHM
SAN FRANCISCO: HARPER & ROW, 1985

LAING, RONALD DAVID

Divided Self
NEW YORK: VIKING PRESS, 1991

R.D. Laing and the Paths of Anti-Psychiatry
ED., BY Z. KOTOWICZ
LONDON: ROUTLEDGE, 1997

The Politics of Experience
NEW YORK: PANTHEON, 1983

LIEDLOFF, JEAN

Continuum Concept
IN SEARCH OF HAPPINESS LOST
NEW YORK: PERSEUS BOOKS, 1986
FIRST PUBLISHED IN 1977

LOWEN, ALEXANDER

Bioenergetics
NEW YORK: COWARD, MCGOEGHAM 1975

Depression and the Body
THE BIOLOGICAL BASIS OF FAITH AND REALITY
NEW YORK: PENGUIN, 1992

Fear of Life
NEW YORK: BIOENERGETIC PRESS, 2003

Honoring the Body
THE AUTOBIOGRAPHY OF ALEXANDER LOWEN
NEW YORK: BIOENERGETIC PRESS, 2004

Joy
THE SURRENDER TO THE BODY AND TO LIFE
NEW YORK: PENGUIN, 1995

Love and Orgasm
NEW YORK: MACMILLAN, 1965

Love, Sex and Your Heart
NEW YORK: BIOENERGETICS PRESS, 2004

Narcissism: Denial of the True Self
NEW YORK: MACMILLAN, COLLIER BOOKS, 1983

Pleasure: A Creative Approach to Life
NEW YORK: BIOENERGETICS PRESS, 2004
FIRST PUBLISHED IN 1970

The Language of the Body
PHYSICAL DYNAMICS OF CHARACTER STRUCTURE
NEW YORK: BIOENERGETICS PRESS, 2006

MILLER, ALICE

Four Your Own Good
HIDDEN CRUELTY IN CHILD-REARING AND THE ROOTS OF VIOLENCE
NEW YORK: FARRAR, STRAUS & GIROUX, 1983

Pictures of a Childhood
NEW YORK: FARRAR, STRAUS & GIROUX, 1986

The Drama of the Gifted Child
IN SEARCH FOR THE TRUE SELF
TRANSLATED BY RUTH WARD
NEW YORK: BASIC BOOKS, 1996

Thou Shalt Not Be Aware
SOCIETY'S BETRAYAL OF THE CHILD
NEW YORK: NOONDAY, 1998

The Political Consequences of Child Abuse
IN: THE JOURNAL OF PSYCHOHISTORY 26, 2 (FALL 1998)

MOORE, THOMAS

Care of the Soul
A GUIDE FOR CULTIVATING DEPTH AND SACREDNESS IN EVERYDAY LIFE
NEW YORK: HARPER & COLLINS, 1994

REICH, WILHELM

Children of the Future
ON THE PREVENTION OF SEXUAL PATHOLOGY
NEW YORK: FARRAR, STRAUS & GIROUX, 1983
FIRST PUBLISHED IN 1950

CORE (Cosmic Orgone Engineering)
PART I, SPACE SHIPS, DOR AND DROUGHT
©1984, ORGONE INSTITUTE PRESS
XEROX COPY FROM THE WILHELM REICH MUSEUM

Early Writings 1
NEW YORK: FARRAR, STRAUS & GIROUX, 1975

Ether, God & Devil & Cosmic Superimposition
NEW YORK: FARRAR, STRAUS & GIROUX, 1972
ORIGINALLY PUBLISHED IN 1949

Genitality in the Theory and Therapy of Neurosis
©1980 BY MARY BOYD HIGGINS AS DIRECTOR OF THE WILHELM REICH INFANT
TRUST

CONTEXTUAL BIBLIOGRAPHY

People in Trouble
©1974 BY MARY BOYD HIGGINS AS DIRECTOR OF THE WILHELM REICH INFANT TRUST

Record of a Friendship
THE CORRESPONDENCE OF WILHELM REICH AND A. S. NEILL
NEW YORK, FARRAR, STRAUS & GIROUX, 1981

Selected Writings
AN INTRODUCTION TO ORGONOMY
NEW YORK: FARRAR, STRAUS & GIROUX, 1973

The Bioelectrical Investigation of Sexuality and Anxiety
NEW YORK: FARRAR, STRAUS & GIROUX, 1983
ORIGINALLY PUBLISHED IN 1935

The Bion Experiments
REPRINTED IN *SELECTED WRITINGS*
NEW YORK: FARRAR, STRAUS & GIROUX, 1973

The Function of the Orgasm (The Orgone, Vol. 1)
ORGONE INSTITUTE PRESS, NEW YORK, 1942

The Cancer Biopathy (The Orgone, Vol. 2)
NEW YORK: FARRAR, STRAUS & GIROUX, 1973

The Invasion of Compulsory Sex Morality
NEW YORK: FARRAR, STRAUS & GIROUX, 1971
ORIGINALLY PUBLISHED IN 1932

The Leukemia Problem: Approach
©1951, ORGONE INSTITUTE PRESS
COPYRIGHT RENEWED 1979
XEROX COPY FROM THE WILHELM REICH MUSEUM

The Mass Psychology of Fascism
NEW YORK: FARRAR, STRAUS & GIROUX, 1970
ORIGINALLY PUBLISHED IN 1933

The Orgone Energy Accumulator
ITS SCIENTIFIC AND MEDICAL USE
©1951, 1979, ORGONE INSTITUTE PRESS
XEROX COPY FROM THE WILHELM REICH MUSEUM

The Schizophrenic Split
©1945, 1949, 1972 BY MARY BOYD HIGGINS AS DIRECTOR OF THE
WILHELM REICH INFANT TRUST
XEROX COPY FROM THE WILHELM REICH MUSEUM

The Sexual Revolution
©1945, 1962 BY MARY BOYD HIGGINS AS DIRECTOR OF THE WILHELM REICH
INFANT TRUST

REID, DANIEL P.

The Tao of Health, Sex & Longevity
A MODERN PRACTICAL GUIDE TO THE ANCIENT WAY
NEW YORK: SIMON & SCHUSTER, 1989

Guarding the Three Treasures
THE CHINESE WAY OF HEALTH
NEW YORK: SIMON & SCHUSTER, 1993

ROSEN, SYDNEY (ED.)

My Voice Will Go With You
THE TEACHING TALES OF MILTON H. ERICKSON
NEW YORK: NORTON & CO., 1991

STEIN, ROBERT M.

Redeeming the Inner Child in Marriage and Therapy
IN: RECLAIMING THE INNER CHILD
ED. BY JEREMIAH ABRAMS
NEW YORK: TARCHER/PUTNAM, 1990, 261 FF.

STEINER, RUDOLF

Theosophy
AN INTRODUCTION TO THE SPIRITUAL PROCESSES IN HUMAN LIFE
AND IN THE COSMOS
NEW YORK: ANTHROPOSOPHIC PRESS, 1994

STONE, HAL & STONE, SIDRA

Embracing Our Selves
THE VOICE DIALOGUE MANUAL
SAN RAFAEL, CA: NEW WORLD LIBRARY, 1989

SZASZ, THOMAS

The Myth of Mental Illness
NEW YORK: HARPER & ROW, 1984

TART, CHARLES T.

Altered States of Consciousness
A BOOK OF READINGS
HOBOKEN, N.J.: WILEY & SONS, 1969

WHAT THE BLEEP DO WE KNOW!?

See Arntz, William

WHITFIELD, CHARLES L.

Healing the Child Within
DEERFIELD BEACH, FL: HEALTH COMMUNICATIONS, 1987

Personal Notes

www.ingramcontent.com/pod-product-compliance
Lightning Source LLC
Chambersburg PA
CBHW020902310526
45786CB00018B/1585